A CONNECTICUT YANKEE IN KING ARTHUR'S COURT

Hank Morgan is the boss of a factory in Connecticut, USA. One day in 1879 Hank is working in his office. One of his workers comes in and says, 'Come quickly, Boss! Two men are fighting.' Hank wants to stop the fight, but one of the workers hits him on the head, he sees stars and he closes his eyes.

Suddenly he is in England, and the year is 528 – a dangerous time. He goes to Camelot and he meets King Arthur. But King Arthur is not happy. 'You must die at twelve o'clock on the twenty-first of June,' he says to Hank.

What can Hank do? How can he go home? Before he can get answers to these questions, there are many adventures to come . . .

OXFORD BOOKWORMS LIBRARY

Classics

A Connecticut Yankee in King Arthur's Court

Starter (250 headwords)

MARK TWAIN

A Connecticut Yankee in King Arthur's Court

Retold by
Alan Hines

Illustrated by
Thomas Sperling

OXFORD UNIVERSITY PRESS

OXFORD
UNIVERSITY PRESS

Great Clarendon Street, Oxford OX2 6DP

Oxford University Press is a department of the University of Oxford.
It furthers the University's objective of excellence in research, scholarship,
and education by publishing worldwide in

Oxford New York

Auckland Cape Town Dar es Salaam Hong Kong Karachi
Kuala Lumpur Madrid Melbourne Mexico City Nairobi
New Delhi Shanghai Taipei Toronto

With offices in

Argentina Austria Brazil Chile Czech Republic France Greece
Guatemala Hungary Italy Japan Poland Portugal Singapore
South Korea Switzerland Thailand Turkey Ukraine Vietnam

OXFORD and OXFORD ENGLISH are registered trade marks of
Oxford University Press in the UK and in certain other countries

ISBN: 978 0 19 423411 5

Printed in China

Word count (main text): 890

For more information on the Oxford Bookworms Library, visit
www.oup.com/elt/gradedreaders

This book is printed on paper from certified and well-managed sources.

CONTENTS

At last! The Boss is here!

There's no water and Merlin can't help.

Merlin can't bring the water again. I can, but I need time – and my things.

Clarence, bring me my things and two of my helpers.

Sir Sagramor comes back.

Sir Sagramor wants to fight you.

Look at him. I want to laugh!

Hank Morgan wakes up at the beginning of the twentieth century. He is now seventy years old. His American family is with him.

GLOSSARY

adventure *(n)* something you do that is different and
  exciting
boss the person who tells workers what to do
bugle a musical instrument
century a hundred years
court the place where the king lives
cowboy a person who takes care of cattle,
  usually on horseback
danger something that might hurt you
factory a place where things are made
fight *(n)* something that happens sometimes when you are
  angry or don't agree with someone
knight a person who protects the king and helps people in
  danger
machine a thing with parts that move to make it work;
  it works for people
magic a kind of power that seems to be real but is not
moon a big bright object in the sky at night; it goes around
  the earth
pretend make believe you are doing something
sir a title like Mr
slave someone who must work for no money
weapon something used for fighting

A Connecticut Yankee
in King Arthur's Court

ACTIVITIES

ACTIVITIES

Before Reading

1 **Look at the front cover of the book.**
Now guess the answers to these questions.

1 The main character is Hank Morgan. Hank is…

a ☐ a young man from Connecticut, USA.

b ☐ an old man from sixth-century England.

c ☐ someone from the the future.

2 Most of the story takes place in…

a ☐ another world.

b ☐ America.

c ☐ England.

3 In this story Hank…

a ☐ spends all of his time in prison.

b ☐ has many different experiences.

c ☐ becomes a king.

2 **Read the back cover of the book.**
Guess what happens.

	YES	NO
1 The police arrest Hank for attacking his workers.	☐	☐
2 Hank hurts his head and goes to hospital.	☐	☐
3 Hank's workers kidnap him.	☐	☐
4 Hank travels through time.	☐	☐

ACTIVITIES

While Reading

1 Match the words with the pictures.

a ☐ 'He says you must die.
He wants to fight again.'

b ☐ 'Merlin can't bring the
water again. I can, but I
need time – and my things.'

c ☐ 'They want to kill us
today because a slave is
missing.'

d ☐ 'What year is it?'

2 Read pages 1–6.
Are these sentences true (T) or false (F)?

	T	F
1 When Hank wakes up, he wants to call the police.	☐	☐
2 Merlin likes Hank.	☐	☐
3 The people think that Hank makes the sun go away.	☐	☐
4 Merlin gives Hank a new name.	☐	☐

3 Read pages 7–12, then answer these questions.

1 What does the Boss need to do before Sir Sagramor comes back?
2 Why does Sandy come to Camelot?
3 Merlin wants to bring the water back – what does he use?
4 What does King Arthur see when he comes to the village?

4 Read pages 13–18. Who says or thinks these words?

1 'When we meet people, remember that you are not the King.'
2 'You are runaway slaves!'
3 'Who wants these slaves for four dollars?'
4 'Clarence, listen to me. The King is in a lot of danger. Bring the knights quickly.'

5 Read pages 19–24, then answer these questions.

1 Who takes the Boss's rope?
2 What new weapon does the Boss have?
3 What sport do English people now play?
4 Who is with Hank Morgan when he dies?

ACTIVITIES

After Reading

1 Put these twelve sentences in the right order to tell the story.

a ☐ Hank is hit on the head at the factory in Connecticut.

b ☐ Dressed as ordinary people, the Boss and King Arthur are sold as slaves.

c ☐ The Boss wakes up in twentieth century America.

d ☐ Merlin uses magic on the Boss to make him sleep.

e ☐ The Boss sets out to help Sandy's village.

f ☐ The Boss repairs the well, just as King Arthur arrives.

g ☐ The Boss defeats a knight by roping him.

h ☐ Hank becomes the Boss and makes changes in Camelot.

i ☐ The Boss and King Arthur are saved by knights from Camelot.

j ☐ Hank's 'miracle' with the sun makes him a hero.

k ☐ The King tells Hank that he must die.

l ☐ The year is 528 when Hank wakes up in England.

2 Answer these questions.

Who . . .

a . . . hits Hank on the head?

b . . . comes to Camelot and asks for help?

c . . . does Hank call in Camelot when he needs help with the water?

d . . . wants to get rid of the Boss?

What . . .

f . . . does Hank see first when he wakes up in the year 528?

g . . . does Sandy think about Hank on their way to her village?

h . . . do the villagers think about the Boss and King Arthur?

i . . . does the boss change in Camelot?

Where . . .

j . . . does Hank Morgan work?

k . . . does King Arthur send Hank while he waits to die?

l . . . are the Boss and Arthur when the villagers catch them?

m . . . does the Boss fight the knight?

ABOUT THE AUTHOR

Mark Twain's real name was Samuel Clemens. He was born in Florida, a town in Missouri, USA, in 1835 and he then lived in Hannibal, Missouri. When he was twelve, his father died, and he went out to work. He began to write for his brother's newspaper and later he wrote for newspapers in Nevada and California. From 1857 to 1861, he was a river-pilot, guiding river boats on the great Mississippi river.

He started to write books of stories in 1867 and became famous for making people laugh. *The Adventures of Tom Sawyer* (1876) and *Huckleberry Finn* (1884) are his two most famous books. Many of the people and places in these stories are from the years when Mark Twain was a boy in Hannibal. Mark Twain wrote many books. Some of them were important, some not so important, and he travelled to many English-speaking countries, talking about his work. Sadly, he had money problems, and his wife and two of his three daughters died before him, so his life was difficult and unhappy when he was older. He died in 1910.

OXFORD BOOKWORMS LIBRARY

Classics • Crime & Mystery • Factfiles • Fantasy & Horror
Human Interest • Playscripts • Thriller & Adventure
True Stories • World Stories

The OXFORD BOOKWORMS LIBRARY provides enjoyable reading in English, with a wide range of classic and modern fiction, non-fiction, and plays. It includes original and adapted texts in seven carefully graded language stages, which take learners from beginner to advanced level. An overview is given on the next pages.

All Stage 1 titles are available as audio recordings, as well as over eighty other titles from Starter to Stage 6. All Starters and many titles at Stages 1 to 4 are specially recommended for younger learners. Every Bookworm is illustrated, and Starters and Factfiles have full-colour illustrations.

The OXFORD BOOKWORMS LIBRARY also offers extensive support. Each book contains an introduction to the story, notes about the author, a glossary, and activities. Additional resources include tests and worksheets, and answers for these and for the activities in the books. There is advice on running a class library, using audio recordings, and the many ways of using Oxford Bookworms in reading programmes. Resource materials are available on the website <www.oup.com/elt/gradedreaders>.

The *Oxford Bookworms Collection* is a series for advanced learners. It consists of volumes of short stories by well-known authors, both classic and modern. Texts are not abridged or adapted in any way, but carefully selected to be accessible to the advanced student.

You can find details and a full list of titles in the *Oxford Bookworms Library Catalogue* and *Oxford English Language Teaching Catalogues*, and on the website <www.oup.com/elt/gradedreaders>.

THE OXFORD BOOKWORMS LIBRARY
GRADING AND SAMPLE EXTRACTS

STARTER • 250 HEADWORDS

present simple – present continuous – imperative –
can/cannot, must – *going to* (future) – simple gerunds ...

Her phone is ringing – but where is it?

Sally gets out of bed and looks in her bag. No phone. She looks under the bed. No phone. Then she looks behind the door. There is her phone. Sally picks up her phone and answers it. *Sally's Phone*

STAGE 1 • 400 HEADWORDS

... past simple – coordination with *and, but, or* –
subordination with *before, after, when, because, so* ...

I knew him in Persia. He was a famous builder and I worked with him there. For a time I was his friend, but not for long. When he came to Paris, I came after him – I wanted to watch him. He was a very clever, very dangerous man. *The Phantom of the Opera*

STAGE 2 • 700 HEADWORDS

... present perfect – *will* (future) – *(don't) have to, must not, could* –
comparison of adjectives – simple *if* clauses – past continuous –
tag questions – *ask/tell* + infinitive ...

While I was writing these words in my diary, I decided what to do. I must try to escape. I shall try to get down the wall outside. The window is high above the ground, but I have to try. I shall take some of the gold with me – if I escape, perhaps it will be helpful later. *Dracula*

STAGE 3 • 1000 HEADWORDS

… should, may – present perfect continuous – *used to* – past perfect –
causative – relative clauses – indirect statements …

Of course, it was most important that no one should see
Colin, Mary, or Dickon entering the secret garden. So Colin
gave orders to the gardeners that they must all keep away
from that part of the garden in future. ***The Secret Garden***

STAGE 4 • 1400 HEADWORDS

… past perfect continuous – passive (simple forms) –
would conditional clauses – indirect questions –
relatives with *where/when* – gerunds after prepositions/phrases …

I was glad. Now Hyde could not show his face to the world
again. If he did, every honest man in London would be proud
to report him to the police. ***Dr Jekyll and Mr Hyde***

STAGE 5 • 1800 HEADWORDS

… future continuous – future perfect –
passive (modals, continuous forms) –
would have conditional clauses – modals + perfect infinitive …

If he had spoken Estella's name, I would have hit him. I was so
angry with him, and so depressed about my future, that I could
not eat the breakfast. Instead I went straight to the old house.
Great Expectations

STAGE 6 • 2500 HEADWORDS

… passive (infinitives, gerunds) – advanced modal meanings –
clauses of concession, condition

When I stepped up to the piano, I was confident. It was as if I
knew that the prodigy side of me really did exist. And when I
started to play, I was so caught up in how lovely I looked that
I didn't worry how I would sound. ***The Joy Luck Club***

BOOKWORMS · CLASSICS · STARTER

The Ransom of Red Chief

O. HENRY

Retold by Paul Shipton

Bill and Sam arrive in the small American town of Summit with only two hundred dollars, but they need more and Sam has an idea for making a lot of money. When things start to go very wrong, both men soon regret their visit – and the idea.

BOOKWORMS · HUMAN INTEREST · STARTER

King Arthur

JANET HARDY-GOULD

It is the year 650 in England. There is war everywhere because the old king is dead and he has no son. Only when the new king comes can the fighting stop and the strange, magical story of King Arthur begin. But first, Merlin the ancient magician has to find a way of finding the next king . . .

BOOKWORMS · HUMAN INTEREST · STARTER

Robin Hood

JOHN ESCOTT

'You're a brave man, but I am afraid for you,' says Lady Marian to Robin of Locksley. She is afraid because Robin does not like Prince John's new taxes and wants to do something for the poor people of Nottingham. When Prince John hears this, Robin is suddenly in danger – great danger.

BOOKWORMS · FANTASY & HORROR · STARTER

Starman

PHILLIP BURROWS AND MARK FOSTER

The empty centre of Australia. The sun is hot and there are not many people. And when Bill meets a man, alone, standing on an empty road a long way from anywhere, he is surprised and worried.

And Bill is right to be worried. Because there is something strange about the man he meets. Very strange . . .

BOOKWORMS · CLASSICS · STAGE 1

The Adventures of Tom Sawyer

MARK TWAIN

Retold by Nick Bullard

Tom Sawyer does not like school. He does not like work, and he never wants to get out of bed in the morning. But he likes swimming and fishing, and having adventures with his friends. And he has a lot of adventures. One night, he and his friend Huck Finn go to the graveyard to look for ghosts.

They don't see any ghosts that night. They see something worse than a ghost – much, much worse . . .

BOOKWORMS · FANTASY & HORROR · STAGE 1

The Wizard of Oz

L. FRANK BAUM

Retold by Rosemary Border

Dorothy lives in Kansas, USA, but one day a cyclone blows her and her house to a strange country called Oz. There, Dorothy makes friends with the Scarecrow, the Tin Man, and the Cowardly Lion.

But she wants to go home to Kansas. Only one person can help her, and that is the country's famous Wizard. So Dorothy and her friends take the yellow brick road to the Emerald City, to find the Wizard of Oz . . .